Grammaropolis
PRESENTS

T0159987

SENTENCE FACTORY

EST. 2014

Student Workbook

GRADES 3-5

written by
THE MAYOR OF GRAMMAROPOLIS

HOUSTON

Edited by Christopher Knight
Cover and Interior Design by Mckee Frazior
Character Design by Powerhouse Animation & Mckee Frazior

ISBN: 9781644420195
Copyright © 2020 by Grammaropolis LLC
Illustrations copyright © 2020 by Grammaropolis LLC
All rights reserved.
Published by Six Foot Press
Printed in the U.S.A.

Grammaropolis.com
Six Foot Press.com

Table of Contents

Table of Contents

For information on how Grammaropolis correlates to state standards, please visit us online at edu.grammaropolis.com

SENTENCE ⬡ FACTORY

FROM THE DESK OF THE MAYOR

There's a reason students can instantly recall everything that happened in their favorite movies but struggle to retain much of the important information you're trying to cover in school: people are hard-wired to remember what we connect with on an emotional level.

That's why grammar is so hard to teach. (As a former grammar teacher myself, I know firsthand.) Traditional materials are dry, abstract, and lifeless. There's nothing to connect with. Put simply, grammar is boring.

But it doesn't have to be! Our story-based approach combines traditional instruction with original narrative content, appealing to different learning styles and encouraging students to make a deeper connection with the elements of grammar.

In Grammaropolis, adverbs don't just modify verbs; adverbs are bossy! They tell the verbs **where** to go, **when** to leave, and **how** to get there. A pronoun doesn't just replace a noun; Roger the pronoun is a shady character who's always trying to trick Nelson the noun into giving up his spot.

And it works! Our mobile apps have already been downloaded over 2.5 million times, and thousands of schools and districts use our web-based site license. In other words, we don't skimp on the vegetables; we just make them taste good.

Thanks so much for visiting Grammaropolis. I hope you enjoy your stay!

– *The Mayor*

Meet the Parts of Speech!

Nouns

name a person, place, thing, or idea.

Verbs

express action or a state of being.

Adverbs

modify a verb, an adjective, or another adverb.

Adjectives

modify a noun or pronoun.

Prepositions

show a logical relationship or locate an object in time or space.

Pronouns

take the place of one or more nouns or pronouns.

Interjections

express strong or mild emotion.

Conjunctions

join words or word groups.

SENTENCE ⚙ FACTORY

Meet the Punctuation Department!

Welcome to the Sentence Factory!

The Parts of the Sentence

 Meet the **Parts of Speech** 8 POPULATION

+

 **P**unctuate **This**

=

 SENTENCE FACTORY EST. 2014

PARTS OF SPEECH　　**PUNCTUATION**　　**SENTENCES**

 PRONOUN　 ACTION VERB　 PERIOD

It　rained　.

SUBJECT　PREDICATE　PUNCTUATION

 LINKING VERB　 PRONOUN　ADJECTIVE　NOUN　QUESTION MARK

Are　you　my　teacher　?

SUBJECT　PREDICATE NOMINATIVE　PUNCTUATION

 PROPER NOUN　 ACTION VERB　 PROPER NOUN　 COMMON NOUN　EXCLAMATION MARK

Dayton　gave　Annie　chocolate　!

SUBJECT　TRANSITIVE VERB　INDIRECT OBJECT　DIRECT OBJECT　PUNCTUATION

Let's bring it all together!

Now that you know the parts of speech and punctuation, it's time to put that knowledge into action. Get ready to produce our town's #1 export: **grammatically correct sentences.**

 SUBORDINATING CONJUNCTION　 COMMA

When　you　tell　jokes　,　I　laugh　.

SUBORDINATE CLAUSE　PUNCTUATION　INDEPENDENT CLAUSE　PUNCTUATION

 PROPER NOUN　 ACTION VERB　 PREPOSITION　 COMMON NOUN　 PERIOD

Susan　ran　to　the　store　.

SUBJECT

OBJECT OF PREPOSITION
PREPOSITIONAL PHRASE　PUNCTUATION

PREDICATE

SENTENCE FACTORY

The Sentence

If all of these components are not present, you don't have a complete sentence!

THE SENTENCE

CHECKLIST FOR A COMPLETE SENTENCE

- ☐ has a subject
- ☐ has a verb
- ☐ expresses a complete thought
- ☐ is punctuated with an end mark
- ☐ begins with a capitalized word

EXAMPLES

Studied for the test.	No subject!
My friend Regina.	No verb!
Because my friend Regina studied.	No complete thought!
My friend Regina studied for the test	No end mark!
my friend Regina studied for the test.	No capitalization!
My friend Regina studied for the test.	It's a sentence!

Types of Sentences

We use different types of sentences for different purposes.

TYPES OF SENTENCES

A **_DECLARATIVE SENTENCE_**
makes a statement and ends with a period.

An **_IMPERATIVE SENTENCE_**
expresses a command or request
and ends with a period or exclamation mark.

An **_INTERROGATIVE SENTENCE_**
asks a question and ends with a question mark.

An **_EXCLAMATORY SENTENCE_**
expresses strong feeling
and ends with an exclamation mark.

EXAMPLES

DECLARATIVE
I will make myself a sandwich.

IMPERATIVE
Make yourself a sandwich right now!
Please make yourself a sandwich.

INTERROGATIVE
Did you make yourself a sandwich?

EXCLAMATORY
You made yourself a sandwich!

Types of Sentences

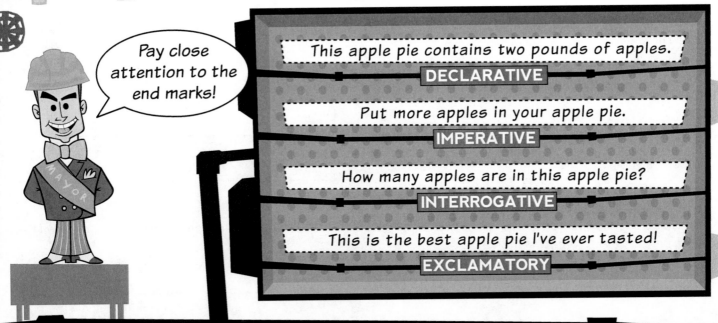

Pay close attention to the end marks!

This apple pie contains two pounds of apples.
DECLARATIVE

Put more apples in your apple pie.
IMPERATIVE

How many apples are in this apple pie?
INTERROGATIVE

This is the best apple pie I've ever tasted!
EXCLAMATORY

Let's practice!

Instructions:
Tell whether the sentences below are declarative, imperative, interrogative, or exclamatory.

EXAMPLE:

My little sister finally let me borrow her unicorn glitter!   exclamatory

1. Writing notebooks are useful for many people.   _____

2. When do you think our teacher is going to let us leave?   _____

3. Please do not track mud all over my clean white carpet.   _____

4. Give me some of that chocolate cake!   _____

5. I absolutely love that movie!   _____

Your turn!

Instructions:
Write sentences that incorporate the words below. Write only one sentence of each type and label your sentences as declarative, imperative, interrogative, or exclamatory.

1. table _____

2. hat _____

3. phone _____

4. eyes _____

Writing the Types of Sentences

DECLARATIVE SENTENCES:
Write three **declarative** sentences.

1. _____

2. _____

3. _____

IMPERATIVE SENTENCES:
Turn those declarative sentences into **imperative** sentences. You may end these imperative sentences with either periods or exclamation marks.

1. _____

2. _____

3. _____

INTERROGATIVE SENTENCES:
Turn your original declarative sentences into **interrogative** sentences.

1. _____

2. _____

3. _____

EXCLAMATORY SENTENCES:
Turn your original declarative sentences into **exclamatory** sentences.

1. _____

2. _____

3. _____

SENTENCE FACTORY

The Big "Types of Sentences" Quiz!

INSTRUCTIONS: Indicate whether each of the following sentences is **declarative**, **imperative**, **interrogative**, or **exclamatory**.

EXAMPLE:

Please pass me the chocolate sauce as soon as you can.   ___imperative___

1. Do you have any chocolate sauce?   _____

2. Last week, my sister gave me a box of spiders as a joke.   _____

3. That gerbil is riding a skateboard!   _____

4. I have never seen anything like it in my whole life.   _____

5. Do your homework before you try to skateboard like that gerbil.   _____

6. Where can I find more videos of gerbils riding skateboards?   _____

7. Don't even think about training my cat to roller skate.   _____

8. Did I mention how much I love chocolate sauce?   _____

9. I love chocolate sauce.   _____

10. I really love chocolate sauce so much!   _____

Sentence Structures

There are four basic sentence structures, which are various combinations of types of clauses.

SENTENCE STRUCTURES

A **_SIMPLE SENTENCE_**
contains _one_ independent clause.

A **_COMPOUND SENTENCE_**
contains _two or more_ independent clauses
and _no_ subordinate clauses.

A **_COMPLEX SENTENCE_**
contains _one_ independent clause
and _one or more_ subordinate clauses.

A **_COMPOUND/COMPLEX SENTENCE_**
Contains _two or more_ independent clauses
and _at least one_ subordinate clause.

EXAMPLES

SIMPLE

I studied for the test.

COMPOUND

I studied for the test, so I did well.

COMPLEX

Because I wanted to do well, I studied for the test before class started.

COMPOUND/COMPLEX

Before class started, I studied for the test, so I did well.

Sentence Structures

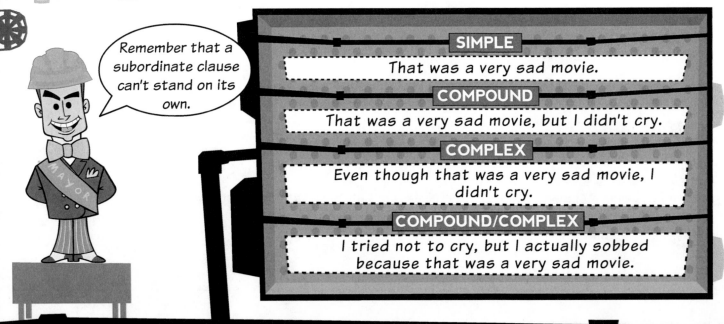

Remember that a subordinate clause can't stand on its own.

SIMPLE
That was a very sad movie.

COMPOUND
That was a very sad movie, but I didn't cry.

COMPLEX
Even though that was a very sad movie, I didn't cry.

COMPOUND/COMPLEX
I tried not to cry, but I actually sobbed because that was a very sad movie.

Let's practice!

Instructions:
Tell whether the sentences below are **simple, compound, complex,** or **compound/complex.**

EXAMPLE:

It's your birthday, so I bought you a gift.   ___compound___

1.   Most of the cars on the road have internal combustion engines. _____

2.   Before James went to bed, he brushed his teeth.   _____

3.   Whenever we meet, Bethany talks about birds, and I take notes.   _____

4.   Whatever you do, don't look down!   _____

5.   My favorite desk is on sale, but I still can't afford it.   _____

Your turn!

Instructions:
Write one of each kind of sentence structure in the spaces provided below.

1. simple   _____

2. compound   _____

3. complex   _____

4. compound/
   complex   _____

Writing the Sentence Structures

SIMPLE SENTENCES:
Write two **simple** sentences.

1. _____

2. _____

COMPOUND SENTENCES:
Add an **independent** clause to each of your **simple** sentences to turn them into **compound** sentences.

1. _____

2. _____

COMPLEX SENTENCES:
Add a **subordinate** clause to each of your **simple** sentences and turn them into **complex** sentences.

1. _____

_____

2. _____

_____

COMPOUND/COMPLEX SENTENCES:
Add a **subordinate** clause to each of your **compound** sentences to turn them into **compound/complex** sentences.

1. _____

_____

2. _____

_____

The Big "Sentence Structures" Quiz!

INSTRUCTIONS: Indicate whether each of the following sentences is **simple**, **compound**, **complex**, or **compound/complex**.

EXAMPLE:

My two cats sleep all day long.   _____simple_____

1.   Sandra went to the store, and she bought some milk.   _____

2.   Sandra went to the store and bought some milk.   _____

3.   Because she was out of milk, Sandra went to the store.   _____

4.   My dad, who never drinks milk, went with Sandra to the store,   _____
     but he refused to pay for her milk.

5.   Although the weather is nice today, I am not going outside   _____
     because I have a terrible headache.

6.   Give it a rest, please.   _____

7.   I was exhausted yesterday, but I still didn't sleep last night.   _____

8.   Annie's computer died during the middle of a test because   _____
     she forgot to plug it in.

9.   Even though Dayton bought his mom a flower, he didn't give   _____
     it to her because he left it on the counter at the flower shop.

10. Go away!   _____

The Subject

> The **subject** is what the sentence is about.

THE SUBJECT

The **SIMPLE SUBJECT**
is the main word or words that the sentence is about.

Your guitar **teacher** plays in a band.

The **COMPLETE SUBJECT**
includes the simple subject and all of its modifiers.

Your guitar teacher plays in a band.

The **COMPOUND SUBJECT**
is two or more subjects that share the same verb.

Your guitar **teacher** and my **uncle** play in the same band.

EXAMPLES

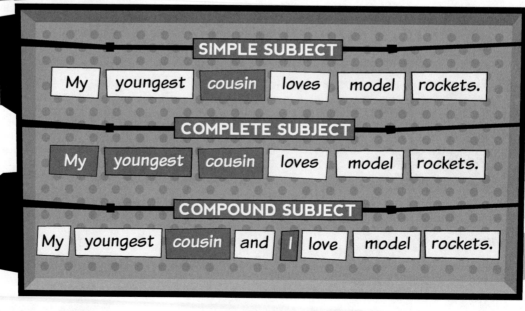

SIMPLE SUBJECT

| My | youngest | cousin | loves | model | rockets. |

COMPLETE SUBJECT

| My | youngest | cousin | loves | model | rockets. |

COMPOUND SUBJECT

| My | youngest | cousin | and | I | love | model | rockets. |

The Simple Subject

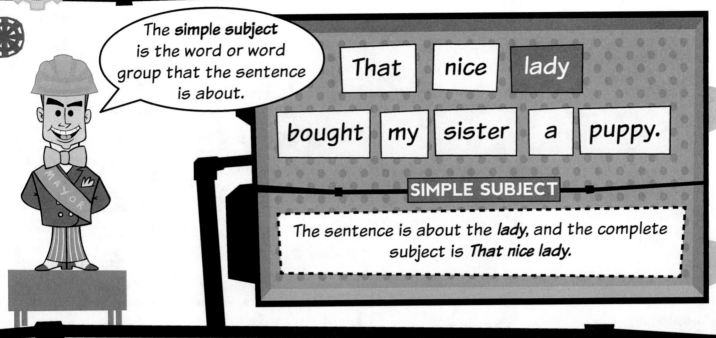

The **simple subject** is the word or word group that the sentence is about.

SIMPLE SUBJECT

The sentence is about the *lady*, and the complete subject is *That nice lady.*

Let's practice!

Instructions:
Underline the complete subject and circle the simple subject in each of the following sentences.

EXAMPLE:

The president of our class gave a great campaign speech.

1. Many birds migrate to warmer climates during the winter months.

2. The new kid in Belinda's class moved to town last week.

3. Our old dishwasher doesn't really do a very good job of washing dishes.

4. Niles's first job was mowing lawns in the neighborhood.

5. Tonight we will all run to the corner store for dessert.

Your turn!

Instructions:
Write sentences with the words below acting as simple subjects. Underline the complete subject of each sentence.

1. friend _____

2. spider _____

3. balloon _____

The Compound Subject

Name:

A **compound subject** is two or more simple subjects that share the same verb.

Zadie | and | her | brother

play | chess | together.

COMPOUND SUBJECT

The sentence is about *Zadie* and her *brother*, and they share the same verb: *play.*

Let's practice!

Instructions:
Underline the complete subject and circle the compound subject in each of the following sentences.

EXAMPLE:
Your dad and my annoying roommate played charades with us last night.

1. French and Spanish are both examples of Romance languages.

2. My little brother and I went to the grocery store together.

3. Mashed potatoes, tacos, and fried shrimp are only some of Lucy's favorite foods.

4. New students and their guardians should submit questions in advance of the meeting.

5. Mr. Lokker and his daughter will be handling the announcements tonight.

Your turn!

Instructions:
Write sentences with each of the words below acting as part of a compound subject. Circle the compound subject and underline the complete subject of each sentence.

1. cars _____

2. book _____

3. mother _____

Writing the Subject

INSTRUCTIONS (PART ONE):
Add your own subjects to the predicates below in order to make complete sentences. Pay attention to subject/verb agreement, and make sure to circle the simple or compound subject in each.

1. _____ will go to the park tomorrow.

2. _____ feels like baking a big cake.

3. _____ gave my kitten a pretty collar.

INSTRUCTIONS (PART TWO):
Write four complete subjects. Circle the simple or compound subject in each.

EXAMPLE: _____ The (twins) down the street _____

1. _____

2. _____

3. _____

4. _____

INSTRUCTIONS (PART THREE):
Choose your favorite of your four subjects from PART TWO. Now write four different sentences using the same subject (your favorite one from Part Two) in every sentence.

1. _____

2. _____

3. _____

4. _____

The Big "Subjects" Quiz!

INSTRUCTIONS: Circle the subject of each sentence and write it in the space provided. Indicate whether it is a **simple subject (S)** or **compound subject (C)**.

EXAMPLE:

My (friend) down the street is going to teach me to play chess.   friend (S)

1.   Pancakes can be incredibly dry when overcooked.   _____

2.   James, Buck, and Yishan are all new to the school this year.   _____

3.   I really want to go play soccer in the park.   _____

4.   Those people have so many pets.   _____

5.   Their cats and dogs actually live in harmony together.   _____

6.   My teacher's tests and quizzes are extra difficult this week.   _____

7.   That chocolate pudding will probably stain this new rug.   _____

8.   Someone please tell me the answer!   _____

9.   In the old days, boxes of chocolate didn't cost so much.   _____

10. You and your younger sister should really get more sleep.   _____

The Predicate

The **predicate** is the part of the sentence that tells what the subject does (with an action verb) or is (with a linking verb).

THE PREDICATE

The **SIMPLE PREDICATE**
is the verb that tells about the subject.

Your guitar teacher **plays** in a band.

The **COMPLETE PREDICATE**
includes the verb all the words that complete its meaning.

Your guitar teacher **plays in a band.**

The **COMPOUND PREDICATE**
is two or more verbs that share the same subject.

Your guitar teacher **teaches** lessons and **plays** in a band.

EXAMPLES

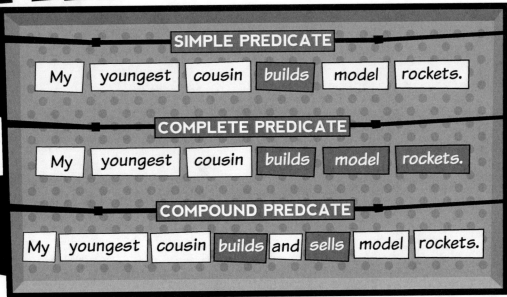

SIMPLE PREDICATE

My | youngest | cousin | builds | model | rockets.

COMPLETE PREDICATE

My | youngest | cousin | builds | model | rockets.

COMPOUND PREDCATE

My | youngest | cousin | builds | and | sells | model | rockets.

The Simple Predicate

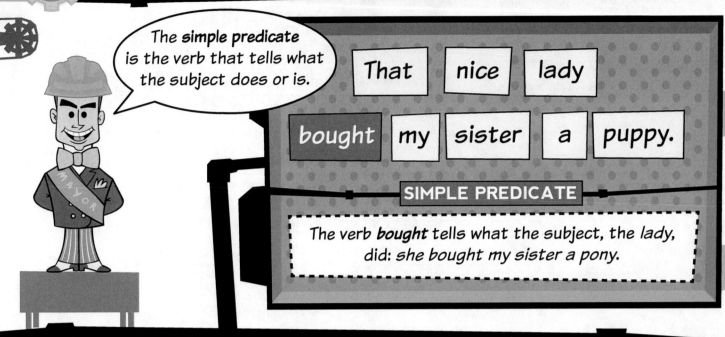

The simple predicate is the verb that tells what the subject does or is.

That | nice | lady

bought | my | sister | a | puppy.

SIMPLE PREDICATE

*The verb **bought** tells what the subject, the lady, did: she bought my sister a pony.*

Let's practice!

Instructions:
Underline the complete predicate and circle the simple predicate in each of the following sentences.

EXAMPLE:

My neighbor's dog barked at me.

1. Computers are sometimes very difficult to work with.

2. My son likes playing with the other children in our neighborhood.

3. The most delicious meal in the world is a bowl of really good cereal.

4. I love listening to people sing at the top of their lungs.

5. At the end of the day, we all went to sleep.

Your turn!

Instructions:
Write sentences with the words below acting as simple predicates. Underline the complete predicate of each sentence.

1. jumped _____

2. will eat _____

3. studies _____

The Compound Predicate

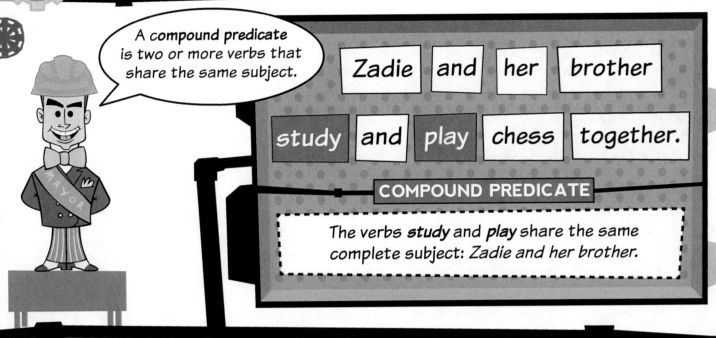

A *compound predicate* is two or more verbs that share the same subject.

Zadie and her brother study and play chess together.

COMPOUND PREDICATE

The verbs **study** and **play** share the same complete subject: *Zadie and her brother.*

Let's practice!

Instructions:
Underline the complete predicate and circle the compound predicate in each of the following sentences.

EXAMPLE:
The little fox jumped over the fence and ran into the forest.

1. The energetic puppy barked at me and licked my face.

2. Gracia did her homework and practiced on the piano.

3. For his allowance, Nelson scrubs the counters, washes dishes, and takes out the trash.

4. Two lucky winners met the rock star and watched her concert from the front row.

5. My neighbor bangs on the drums and plays loud music every night.

Your turn!

Instructions:
Write sentences with each of the verbs below acting as part of a compound predicate. Circle the compound predicate and underline the complete predicate of each sentence.

1. smile _____

2. read _____

3. fall _____

Writing the Predicate

INSTRUCTIONS (PART ONE):

Add your own predicates to the subjects below in order to make complete sentences. Pay attention to subject/verb agreement, and make sure to circle the simple or compound predicate in each.

1. _A polar bear named Francisco_ _____

2. _The girl in the grade ahead of me_ _____

3. _Gianna's favorite song of the year_ _____

INSTRUCTIONS (PART TWO):

Write four complete predicates. Circle the simple or compound predicate in each.

EXAMPLE: _____ (saved) every single one of Kendra's letters. _____

1. _____

2. _____

3. _____

4. _____

INSTRUCTIONS (PART THREE):

Choose your favorite of your four predicates from PART TWO. Now write four different sentences using the same predicate (your favorite one from Part Two) in every sentence.

1. _____

2. _____

3. _____

4. _____

The Big "Predicates" Quiz!

Name:

INSTRUCTIONS: Circle the predicate of each sentence and write it in the space provided. Indicate whether it is a **simple predicate (S)** or **compound predicate (C)**.

EXAMPLE:

My medicine (tastes) like expired milk and rotten vegetables.   __tastes (S)__

1. The two-month-old puppy yipped at me and chewed my shoes.   _____

2. I never saw my best friend's favorite movie.   _____

3. Samantha and Jacqueline will be supportive of each other.   _____

4. Kylo thought long and hard about what to do.   _____

5. Due to a nagging knee injury, I no longer run or jog.   _____

6. Sometimes the world seems so complicated to me.   _____

7. Henry, the kid down the street, will bake me a cake tomorrow.   _____

8. Hey! Be quiet and sit down right now!   _____

9. There are only two correct ways to poach an egg.   _____

10. Hank and I watched movies and ate popcorn all night.   _____

Direct Objects & Indirect Objects

DIRECT & INDIRECT OBJECTS

DIRECT OBJECT
My father made **panckakes**.
Kevin tossed the **ball**.
I left extremely specific **instructions** yesterday.

INDIRECT OBJECT
My father made **me** pancakes.
Kevin tossed **Shondra** the ball.
I left the **students** extremely specific instructions.

A **direct object** is a noun or pronoun that receives the primary action of the verb.

An **indirect object** is a noun or pronoun that receives the action of the verb through the direct object.

Direct objects and indirect objects always come after transitive action verbs.

PRO TIP

EXAMPLES

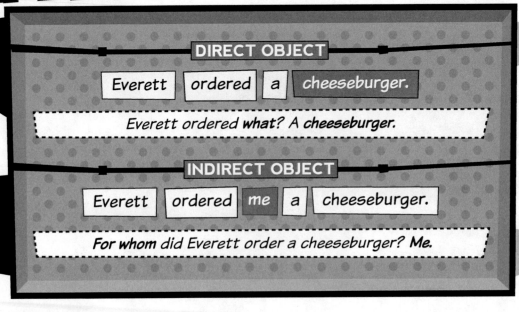

DIRECT OBJECT

| Everett | ordered | a | cheeseburger. |

*Everett ordered **what**? A **cheeseburger**.*

INDIRECT OBJECT

| Everett | ordered | me | a | cheeseburger. |

*For **whom** did Everett order a cheeseburger? **Me**.*

Direct Objects

DIRECT OBJECTS

A **direct object** receives the primary action of the verb.

Seamus wrote his English **paper**.

Paper is the direct object because it receives the action of the verb "wrote". It tells **what** Seamus wrote.

The birds tweeted a lovely **melody** last night at dusk.

Melody is the direct object because it receives the action of the verb "tweeted". It tells **what** the birds tweeted.

It's called a **direct object** because it *directly* receives the action of the verb.

A direct object can only come after a **transitive** verb.

PRO TIP

EXAMPLES

Dayton | and | Annie | did | their | homework.

Dayton and Annie did **what?** Their **homework.**

We | won | the | game

We won **what?** The **game.**

I | scared | my | sister | last | night.

I scared **whom** last night? My **sister.**

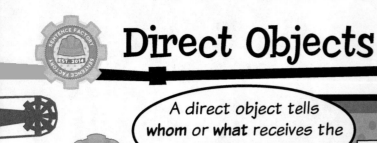

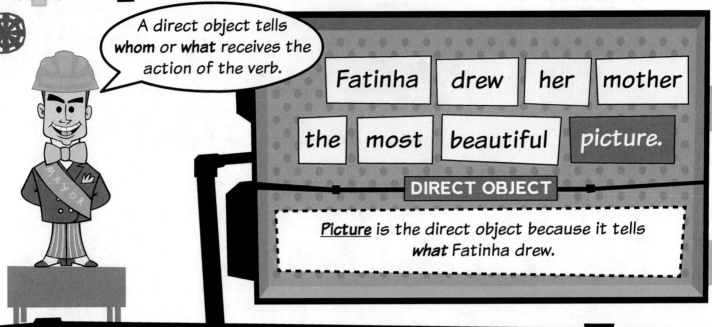

A direct object tells **whom** or **what** receives the action of the verb.

Fatinha drew her mother the most beautiful picture.

DIRECT OBJECT

<u>Picture</u> is the direct object because it tells **what** Fatinha drew.

Let's practice!

Instructions:
Underline the direct object in each of the following sentences.

EXAMPLE:

Marcus gave his teacher an enormous red <u>apple</u>.

1. I don't have any homework today!

2. We went to the park and played soccer.

3. Henrietta's friends pooled their money together.

4. Dayton spends all his time in front of the computer.

5. Let's all take the test before the end of the day.

Your turn!

Instructions:
Write sentences using the words provided as direct objects. Remember to underline the direct objects when you use them.

1. clue _____

2. watch _____

3. shovel _____

Writing Direct Objects

INSTRUCTIONS (PART ONE):
Fill in the blanks with the direct objects of your choice.

1. Charles bought his little sister a _____ .

2. Lissa and her best friend baked _____ for their teacher's birthday.

3. When we all get out of school tomorrow, we can play _____ until it gets dark.

INSTRUCTIONS (PART TWO):
Write sentences using the following words as direct objects.

1. pizza _____

2. shirt _____

3. light _____

4. answer _____

5. bell _____

INSTRUCTIONS (PART THREE):
Write sentences that contain direct objects. Be sure to circle the direct objects you use.

1. _____

2. _____

3. _____

4. _____

INSTRUCTIONS: Underline the direct object in each of the following sentences, and then write it in the space provided. If there is no direct object, write "NONE".

EXAMPLE:

Nobody ever taught me the <u>rules</u> of the game. _____rules_____

1. I have never understood my sister. _____

2. Kev and his little brother ate my entire stash of gummi bears. _____

3. Wash the dishes before you go upstairs. _____

4. Your room kind of smells like potato chips. _____

5. Devon gave me a hard time yesterday for dropping the pan. _____

6. Come here right away, or I will be mad at you. _____

7. The keyboard made an awful sound whenever I typed. _____

8. This test is really hard for me, but I will give it my best effort. _____

9. Sandwiches with sprouts taste better to me. _____

10. Go ahead, give my sandwich a try. _____

Indirect Objects

An **indirect object** receives action of the verb through the direct object.

INDIRECT OBJECTS

I gave my <u>desk</u> a thorough cleaning.

*<u>Desk</u> is the indirect object because it tells **to what** I gave a thorough cleaning.*

Gavin threw <u>**Thomas**</u> another cookie.

*<u>**Thomas**</u> is the indirect object because it shows **to whom** Gavin threw the cookie.*

An indirect object tells **to whom/what** or **for whom/what** the action of the verb happens.

Personal pronouns used as direct or indirect objects must be **objective** (him, me, her, them, etc.).

PRO TIP

EXAMPLES

Alexis | baked | me | a | cake.

*Alexis baked a cake for **whom**? Me.*

Matthew | showed | Patricia | and | Del | a | movie.

*To **whom** did Matthew show a movie? **Patricia** and **Del**.*

My | dad | fed | our | puppy | some | kibble.

*To **what** did my dad feed some kibble? Our **puppy**.*

Indirect Objects

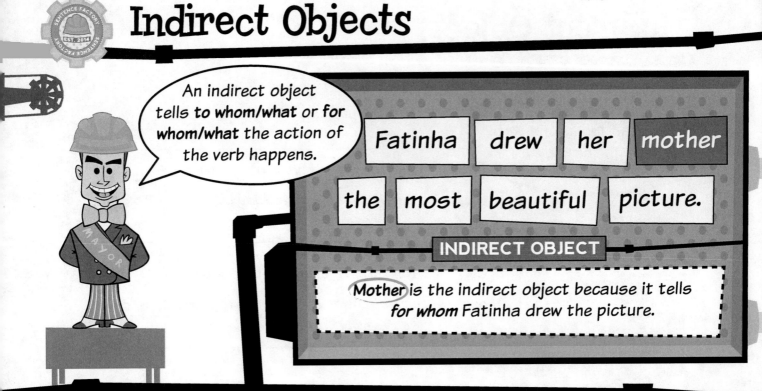

An indirect object tells **to whom/what** or **for whom/what** the action of the verb happens.

Fatinha drew her mother the most beautiful picture.

INDIRECT OBJECT

Mother is the indirect object because it tells **for whom** Fatinha drew the picture.

Let's practice!

Instructions:
Circle the indirect object in each of the following sentences.

EXAMPLE:
Jacob saved his cousin some of his birthday cake.

1. Umi will send me a picture when she gets to the hotel.

2. At the end of class, Mrs. Matterson showed her students a funny movie.

3. A basic rule of thumb is that you should always tell your parents the truth.

4. Vernon is so smart that he taught himself Calculus over the weekend.

5. Before Jake and I brushed our teeth, my mom offered us some candy.

Your turn!

Instructions:
Write sentences using the words provided as indirect objects. Remember that to have an indirect object, the sentence must also contain a direct object.

1. you _____

2. dog _____

3. Sammy _____

Writing Indirect Objects

Name:

INSTRUCTIONS (PART ONE):

Fill in the blanks with the indirect objects of your choice.

1. Franklin gave _____ an entire box of cookies.

2. In a reversal of roles, little Wilhemina taught _____ the rules of the game.

3. Your sister threw _____ a hot potato in plain view of all the adults.

INSTRUCTIONS (PART TWO):

Write sentences using the following words as indirect objects. Remember that you'll need to add direct objects to the sentences, too.

1. **dog** _____

2. **me** _____

3. **ourselves** _____

4. **them** _____

5. **teacher** _____

INSTRUCTIONS (PART THREE):

Write sentences that contain indirect objects. Be sure to underline the indirect objects and circle the direct objects.

1. _____

2. _____

3. _____

4. _____

The Big "Indirect Objects" Quiz!

Name: _____

INSTRUCTIONS: Circle the indirect object in each of the following sentences, and then write it in the space provided. If there is no indirect object, write "NONE".

EXAMPLE:

Hey, man, you've just got to give (yourself) a break.   ___yourself___

1. When I got home from school, my dad made me a sandwich.   _____

2. After I ate my sandwich, my dad made me clean my room.   _____

3. At the end of a long day, I sometimes draw myself a hot bath.   _____

4. The artist drew a picture of himself.   _____

5. Jake bought a box of cookies for his best friend.   _____

6. Jake's best friend bought him a box of lollipops in return.   _____

7. Whenever my dog sees me, he licks me on the face.   _____

8. I usually give my dog a treat before he can lick me.   _____

9. "Save us a seat!" we shouted to Jessica.   _____

10. Blue tape gives our cat a stomach ache if she eats it.   _____

The Big "Direct & Indirect Objects" Quiz!

INSTRUCTIONS: Underline any direct objects and circle any indirect objects in each of the following sentences, and then write them on the lines provided. If there are none, write "NONE".

EXAMPLE:

Our teacher gave (most) of the class the <u>day</u> off.

Direct Object _____ day _____   Indirect Object _____ most _____

1. Please play me a song on the piano.

    Direct Object _____   Indirect Object _____

2. Let's teach the young kids a riddle.

    Direct Object _____   Indirect Object _____

3. Even though it's sometimes difficult, I always tell the truth to my parents.

    Direct Object _____   Indirect Object _____

4. Go over there and toss me the baseball.

    Direct Object _____   Indirect Object _____

5. Should we give each other haircuts?

    Direct Object _____   Indirect Object _____

6. We should give haircuts to each other.

    Direct Object _____   Indirect Object _____

7. At the end of the day, living with integrity is our responsibility.

    Direct Object _____   Indirect Object _____

8. It was a family tradition, so we served everyone a glass of hot chocolate.

    Direct Object _____   Indirect Object _____

9. Put that down over there, okay?

    Direct Object _____   Indirect Object _____

10. We should allow ourselves the freedom to take naps every day.

    Direct Object _____   Indirect Object _____

Subject and Object Complements

A **subject complement** is a noun or adjective that comes after a linking verb and renames or modifies the subject.

An **object complement** is a noun or adjective (or a word that *acts* as a noun or adjective) that renames or modifies a direct object.

SUBJECT & OBJECT COMPLEMENTS

SUBJECT COMPLEMENTS

Your sister is a **doctor**.
"Doctor" is a predicate nominative, a noun that restates the subject.

Your sister is **nice**.
"Nice" is a predicate adjective, an adjective that modifies the subject.

OBJECT COMPLEMENTS

Your sister calls herself **Sandra**.
"Sandra" is a noun that renames "herself" which is a pronoun acting as the direct object of the verb "calls."

An object complement will always come **after** the direct object.

PRO TIP

EXAMPLES

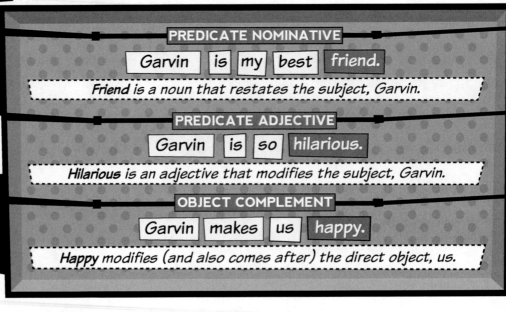

PREDICATE NOMINATIVE

Garvin | is | my | best | friend.

Friend is a noun that restates the subject, Garvin.

PREDICATE ADJECTIVE

Garvin | is | so | hilarious.

Hilarious is an adjective that modifies the subject, Garvin.

OBJECT COMPLEMENT

Garvin | makes | us | happy.

Happy modifies (and also comes after) the direct object, us.

Subject Complements

A **subject complement** will always follow a linking verb.

They're called **predicate adjectives** and **predicate nominatives** because they're in the predicate.

SUBJECT COMPLEMENTS

A **_PREDICATE NOMINATIVE_**
is a noun that comes after a linking verb and renames the subject.

Dr. Anthony is a really friendly <u>dentist</u>.

A **_PREDICATE ADJECTIVE_**
is an adjective that comes after a linking verb and modifies the subject.

Dr. Anthony is really <u>friendly</u>!

EXAMPLES

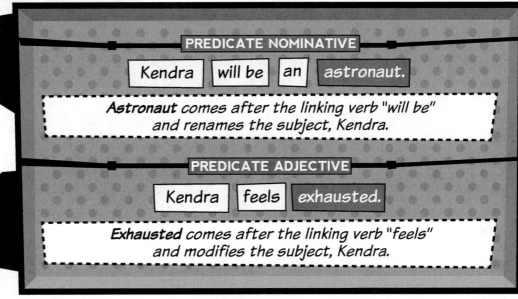

PREDICATE NOMINATIVE

Kendra | will be | an | astronaut.

Astronaut comes after the linking verb "will be" and renames the subject, Kendra.

PREDICATE ADJECTIVE

Kendra | feels | exhausted.

Exhausted comes after the linking verb "feels" and modifies the subject, Kendra.

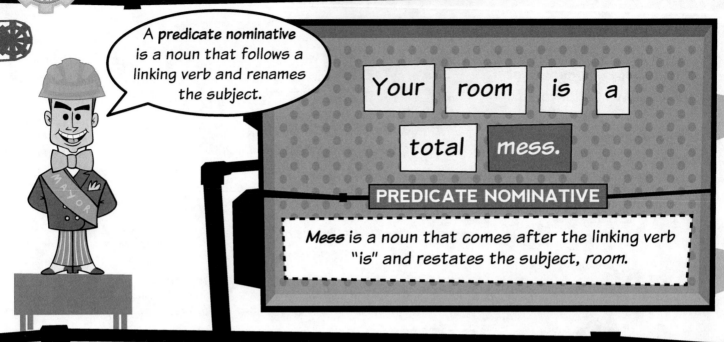

A **predicate nominative** is a noun that follows a linking verb and renames the subject.

Your room is a total mess.

PREDICATE NOMINATIVE

Mess is a noun that comes after the linking verb "is" and restates the subject, *room*.

Let's practice!

Instructions:
Underline the predicate nominative in each of the following sentences.

EXAMPLE:

The book on the table over there is a <u>masterpiece</u>.

1. That guy was a buddy of mine before he stole my bike.

2. If I really work hard, I will become a great teacher.

3. Samantha was always the first person to arrive at school.

4. My best friend in the entire world is that little dog right over there.

5. Gilda was an amazing gymnast from the moment she put on her first leotard.

Your turn!

Instructions:
Write sentences using the words provided as predicate nominatives. Remember to underline the predicate nominatives when you use them.

1. student _____

2. pet _____

3. pudding _____

Predicate Adjectives

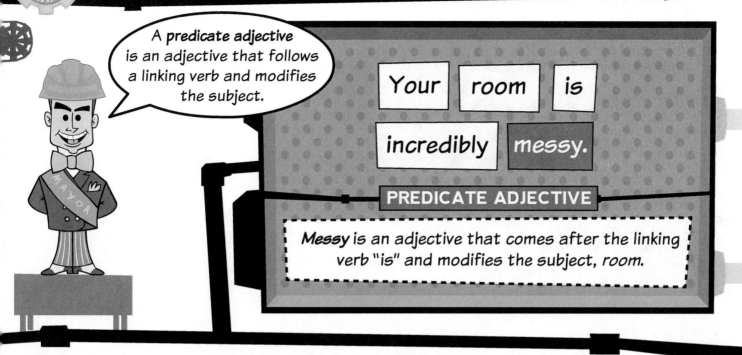

A **predicate adjective** is an adjective that follows a linking verb and modifies the subject.

Your room is incredibly messy.

PREDICATE ADJECTIVE

Messy is an adjective that comes after the linking verb "is" and modifies the subject, *room*.

Let's practice!

Instructions:
Circle the predicate adjective in each of the following sentences.

EXAMPLE:

The pasta at lunch today was (delicious.)

1. I am really sorry, but I don't have any more pudding to share with you.

2. Umm, that cake looks totally overcooked.

3. Carlos became angry when he realized that we had filled his shoes with pebbles.

4. Xavier studied a lot, so he felt confident as he sat down to take the quiz.

5. My neighbor Alia is never ready on time.

Your turn!

Instructions:
Write sentences using the words provided as predicate adjectives. Remember to circle the predicate adjectives when you use them.

1. tired _____

2. honest _____

3. tiny _____

Writing Subject Complements

INSTRUCTIONS (PART ONE):
Fill in the blanks with the subject complements of your choice.

1. After a long day at school, Tonya felt _____.

2. My best friend Devin is _____.

3. Lucy is my favorite _____ in the whole wide world.

INSTRUCTIONS (PART TWO):
Write sentences using the following words as subject complements.

1. **astronaut** _____

2. **silly** _____

3. **winner** _____

4. **frustrated** _____

5. **teacher** _____

INSTRUCTIONS (PART THREE):
Write sentences that contain subject complements. Be sure to circle the subject complements you use.

1. _____

2. _____

3. _____

4. _____

SENTENCE ⚙ FACTORY

The Big "Subject Complements" Quiz!

Name:

INSTRUCTIONS: Circle the subject complement in each sentence, and then write it in the space provided. Indicate whether it is a **predicate nominative** (PN) or **predicate adjective** (PA).

EXAMPLE:

That meatloaf sure smells (delicious!)   delicious (PA)

1. The kid who lives across the street is a real practical joker. _____

2. I will never become a famous actor unless I work harder. _____

3. Your voice sounds a bit scratchy this morning. _____

4. Will you eat that radish if it smells rotten? _____

5. Jake won the lottery because he's just a lucky person. _____

6. Are you serious right now? _____

7. We banged on the door because it was locked. _____

8. If you are hungry, make yourself a quesadilla. _____

9. My neck was so sore after we lifted all those big bags of flour. _____

10. Dayton's great-great-grandfather was a typewriter salesman. _____

Object Complements

An *object complement* renames or modifies a direct object.

An object complement can be a noun, an adjective, or any word *acting* as a noun or an adjective.

OBJECT COMPLEMENTS

AS A NOUN
My neighbor named his son **Reginald**.
"Reginald" is a noun that restates the direct object, son.

AS AN ADJECTIVE
Running makes me **tired**.
"Tired" is an adjective that modifies the direct object, me.

ACTING AS AN ADJECTIVE
Good teaching gets students **engaged**.
"Engaged" is a participle that modifies the direct object, students.

EXAMPLES

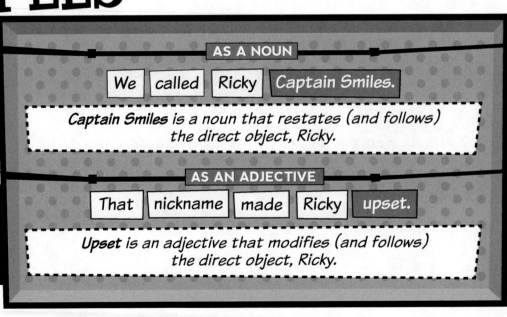

AS A NOUN
| We | called | Ricky | Captain Smiles. |

Captain Smiles is a noun that restates (and follows) the direct object, Ricky.

AS AN ADJECTIVE
| That | nickname | made | Ricky | upset. |

Upset is an adjective that modifies (and follows) the direct object, Ricky.

Object Complements

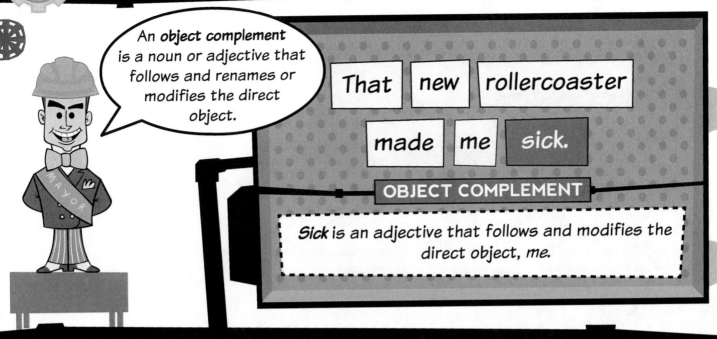

> An **object complement** is a noun or adjective that follows and renames or modifies the direct object.

That | new | rollercoaster

made | me | sick.

OBJECT COMPLEMENT

Sick is an adjective that follows and modifies the direct object, *me*.

Let's practice!

Instructions:
Circle the object complement in each of the following sentences. Then indicate whether it is a noun or an adjective.

EXAMPLE:

That noise in the middle of the night drove me (crazy.)   _adjective_

1. The coach named Franklin captain right before the big game.   _____

2. You can call me overconfident, but I think we're going to win.   _____

3. Pictures of newborn puppies make me happy.   _____

4. Edgar was only a minute late, but the teacher marked him absent.   _____

5. Dottie calls her little brother Dingdong sometimes.   _____

Your turn!

Instructions:
Write sentences with the words provided as direct objects and use object complements to rename or modify them. Remember to circle your object complements.

1. friend _____

2. cat _____

3. silly _____

Writing Object Complements

Name:

INSTRUCTIONS (PART ONE):
Fill in the blanks with the object complements of your choice.

1. I got mad when the bully called me _____ .

2. Moira named her new puppy _____ because it totally looks like one.

3. Seeing famous people running through the park makes my dad _____.

INSTRUCTIONS (PART TWO):
Write sentences using the following words as object complements. Remember that an object complement renames a direct object, so be sure to use direct objects!

1. Harold _____

2. envious _____

3. President _____

4. cheerful _____

5. tired _____

INSTRUCTIONS (PART THREE):
Write sentences that contain object complements. Be sure to use direct objects first, and circle the object complements that rename them.

1. _____

2. _____

3. _____

4. _____

The Big "Object Complements" Quiz!

Name:

INSTRUCTIONS: Circle the object complement in each sentence, and then write it in the space provided. If there is no object complement, write "NONE."

EXAMPLE:

All of your lies are making me (angry,) so please stop lying.   _____angry_____

1. Those fireworks almost gave me a heart attack.   _____

2. Gordon named his daughter Calla because he likes flowers.   _____

3. Eating too many cheeseburgers gives me a tummyache.   _____

4. Eating too many cheeseburgers also makes me happy.   _____

5. You can call me old-fashioned if you want, but I love taffy.   _____

6. The spy's home country branded him a traitor.   _____

7. Really smart computers can turn their screens black, right?   _____

8. The doctors pronounced Johannes healthy after the surgery.   _____

9. Kyrie was voted captain by a unanimous decision.   _____

10. Red pen marks on their papers make my students nervous.   _____

An independent clause is also called the **main clause**.

THE CLAUSE

An **INDEPENDENT CLAUSE** is a group of related words with a subject and a verb that expresses a complete thought.

This blueberry pie is remarkably flavorful.

A **SUBORDINATE CLAUSE** is a group of related words with a subject and a verb that **does not** express a complete thought.

Whenever I eat blueberry pie

A subordinate clause is also called a **dependent** clause because it's not independent.

EXAMPLES

INDEPENDENT CLAUSE

Benji bought his mom a cupcake.

This clause has a subject (Benji) and a verb (bought) and expresses a complete thought.

SUBORDINATE CLAUSE

<u>After he finished school</u>, Benji bought his mom a cupcake.

This clause has a subject (he) and a verb (finished) but does not express a complete thought on its own.

Independent Clauses

An **independent clause** has a subject and a verb and expresses a complete thought.

My little brother wants a toy train for his next birthday.

INDEPENDENT CLAUSE

This clause has a subject (brother) and a verb (wants) and expresses a complete thought.

No more information is necessary for this clause to make sense, so it can stand on its own.

Let's practice!

Instructions:
Circle the subject and underline the verb in each of the clauses below. Then indicate whether the clause is independent or subordinate. (For now, don't worry about proper capitalization and punctuation.)

EXAMPLE:

the weather is unusual for this time of year _____independent_____

1. because Jaime eats salad all the time _____

2. Victoria and her puppy went to the park _____

3. that cheese smells like rotten eggs _____

4. to whom I offered a bite of my sandwich _____

5. the new panda is the cutest animal in the zoo _____

Your turn!

Instructions:
Write three independent clauses with proper punctuation and capitalization. Circle the subjects and underline the verbs.

1. _____

2. _____

3. _____

Writing Independent Clauses

INSTRUCTIONS (PART ONE):
Add independent clauses to the following subordinate clauses to make them complete sentences.

1. Whenever Velma shouts, _____

2. Because I never lie, _____

3. Although it is hot outside,_____

4. So that she will win, _____

5. Wherever I see magic, _____

6. Although Grenny doesn't speak Portuguese, _____

INSTRUCTIONS (PART TWO):
Use one of the sentences above as the first sentence of a story. Make sure that every sentence after the first one is made up of only independent clauses. No subordinate clauses allowed!

_____

_____

_____

_____

_____

_____

_____

The Big "Independent Clauses" Quiz!

Name:

INSTRUCTIONS: Underline the independent clause in each of the word groups below. If there is no independent clause, write NONE in the space provided.

EXAMPLE:

<u>Marcus enjoys playing catch in the park</u> before he eats dinner. _____

1. Jay and Philip are good friends. _____

2. Whenever Belinda comes over to watch television. _____

3. I feel sorry for people who don't know how to bake flan. _____

4. Gavin climbed up to my tree house, but I was nowhere to be found. _____

5. I didn't like the movie, so the best part for me was the very end. _____

6. Come here, sit down, and be quiet. _____

7. So that Sheila knows I care about her, I am writing her a birthday card. _____

8. Molly waited all night for the people across the street to turn off their lights and go to bed. _____

9. I like cheese puffs, but I don't enjoy chocolate mousse. _____

10. Whoever thought it was a good idea in the first place. _____

Subordinate Clauses

THE SUBORDINATE CLAUSE

A subordinate clause is a group of words with a subject and a verb that can't stand on its own.

An **ADJECTIVE CLAUSE** is a subordinate clause that acts as an adjective (modifying a noun or a pronoun).

My dad, **who taught me how to cook**, is visiting tomorrow.

An **ADVERB CLAUSE** is a subordinate clause that acts as an adverb (modifying a verb, adjective, or other adverb).

When my dad arrives tomorrow, we will cook together.

A **NOUN CLAUSE** is a subordinate clause that acts as a noun (a subject, predicate nominative, direct object, indirect object, or object of a preposition).

What we cook tomorrow will be up to him.

A subordinate clause can act as an adjective, an adverb, or a noun.

PRO TIP

EXAMPLES

ADJECTIVE CLAUSE

Jamil saved a seat for her friend, **who was running late**.

This clause acts as an adjective modifying the noun "friend."

ADVERB CLAUSE

Whenever her friend runs late, Jamil saves a seat.

This clause acts as an adverb modifying the verb "saves."

NOUN CLAUSE

Jamil knew **what she needed to do**.

This clause acts as the direct object of the verb "knew."

Adjective Clauses

ADJECTIVE CLAUSE

We went to the town _**where I was born.**_

We went to town, _**where I bought a new coat**_.

An **adjective clause** is a subordinate clause that acts as an adjective, modifying a noun or a pronoun.

An adjective clause begins with a relative pronoun or a relative adverb.

In both cases, the adjective clause modifies "town."

The clause **where I was born** is necessary to understand the meaning of the sentence. That makes it essential.

Non-essential adjective clauses are punctuated with commas.

Let's practice!

Instructions:
Underline the entire adjective clause in each of the sentences below. Then indicate which word the adjective clause modifies.

EXAMPLE:

The only person <u>who can make a more beautiful cake</u> is my sister. _____person_____

1. I want to live in a house that has a view of the mountains. _____

2. Susan, who usually never tells the truth, promised Jake a car. _____

3. My favorite movie, which Lyall has never seen, is showing tonight. _____

4. Let's pay a visit to the kid who lives down the street. _____

5. Danielle just told me everything that she had learned. _____

Your turn!

Instructions:
Rewrite the sentences below, adding an adjective clause to modify the noun in the circle.

1. I like paintings. _____

2. My dad is here today. _____

3. This is the time. _____

Adverb Clauses

An **adverb clause** is a subordinate clause that acts as an adverb, modifying a verb, adjective, or other adverb.

An adverb clause begins with a subordinating conjunction.

ADVERB CLAUSE

**Because it was cold**, I wore a jacket.

I wore a jacket _**because it was cold**_.

An adverb clause can come before or after the independent clause. In both cases, the clause acts as an adverb modifying the verb "wore."

Always put a comma after an introductory adverb clause.

Let's practice!

Instructions:
Underline the entire adverb clause in each of the sentences below. Then indicate which word the adverb clause modifies.

EXAMPLE:

<u>Before he knocked on the door</u>, Asa took a deep breath.   ___took___

1. Because the sun was out, we wore big hats.   _____

2. Nobody will be able to hear you if you don't speak up.   _____

3. Whenever Henri thinks of flowers, his mood improves.   _____

4. Annie and her mother went to the store before it closed.   _____

5. Even if you're feeling lucky, it is a bad idea to play the lottery.   _____

Your turn!

Instructions:
Write three complete sentences by adding independent clauses to the adverb clauses below. Remember that the adverb clause can come either before or after the main clause.

1. after I woke up _____

2. because James laughed _____

3. wherever she looked _____

Noun Clauses

Name:

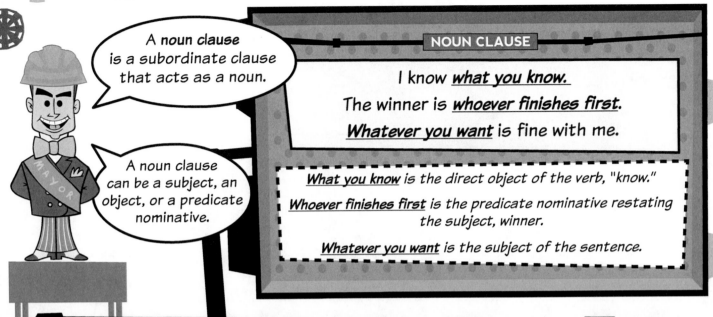

A **noun clause** is a subordinate clause that acts as a noun.

A noun clause can be a subject, an object, or a predicate nominative.

NOUN CLAUSE

I know **what you know.**
The winner is **whoever finishes first.**
Whatever you want is fine with me.

What you know is the direct object of the verb, "know."

Whoever finishes first is the predicate nominative restating the subject, winner.

Whatever you want is the subject of the sentence.

Let's practice!

Instructions:
Underline the entire noun clause in each of the sentences below. Then indicate whether it is acting as the subject, direct object, indirect object, predicate nominative, or object of the preposition in the sentence.

EXAMPLE:
<u>That I am hungry</u> is all I can think about!   <u>   subject   </u>

1. I will give this crayon to whoever wants it.   _____

2. Billy's sister always tells him what she wants.   _____

3. Can you tell me anything about what just happened?   _____

4. Brandon gave whoever would listen to him a popsicle.   _____

5. Whenever we get there will be just in time.   _____

Your turn!

Instructions:
Write three complete sentences that incorporate the noun clauses below as indicated: Subject (S), Direct Object (DO), or Predicate Nominative (PN).

1. what Fran said (S) _____

2. what Fran said (DO) _____

3. what Fran said (PN) _____

Writing Subordinate Clauses

INSTRUCTIONS (PART ONE):

Practice using subordinate clauses by writing two complete sentences that incorporate each of the types of subordinate clauses. Circle the subordinate clause in each sentence.

ADJECTIVE CLAUSES

1. _____

2. _____

ADVERB CLAUSES

1. _____

2. _____

NOUN CLAUSES

1. _____

2. _____

INSTRUCTIONS (PART TWO):

Using one of the sentences above as the first sentence, write a story in which *every sentence includes a subordinate clause.* Underline the subordinate clause in each sentence, marking it as ADJ, ADV, or NOUN.

_____

_____

_____

_____

_____

_____

The Big "Subordinate Clauses" Quiz!

INSTRUCTIONS: Underline the subordinate clause in each of the sentences below and indicate whether it is an **adjective clause (ADJ)**, an **adverb clause (ADV)**, or a **noun clause (N)**.

EXAMPLE:

I know <u>that you are a rocket scientist</u>.   _N_

1. Whenever you feel like it, you should come over.   _____

2. That boy Jason, who never even smiles at me, gave Molly a high five.   _____

3. That we landed on the moon is an established fact.   _____

4. Give me a call as soon as you get home.   _____

5. Stirling did not think that Avery would steal from her.   _____

6. Rick and Connor went to the beach, where they surfed all afternoon.   _____

7. If Xavier actually does his homework tonight, he will get to watch a movie.   _____

8. I had no idea that people in New Mexico ate so much green chile.   _____

9. Quinton slammed the door shut because his little sister was about to barge into his room.   _____

10. The little girl who gave me a chocolate bar lives two houses away from us.   _____

The Big "Clauses" Quiz!

INSTRUCTIONS: Indicate whether each of the word groups below is an **independent clause (IND)**, a **subordinate clause (SUB)**, or **not a clause (NOT)**. If it is a clause, underline the subject and circle the verb.

EXAMPLE:

If <u>you</u> ever ⭕talk to your sister like that again.   <u>SUB</u>

1. Baxter watched the front door very carefully.   _____

2. In order to determine the exact rules of the game.   _____

3. That Susan and her sister arrived this morning.   _____

4. Katherine and Vicky waited until the end of the day before saying anything.   _____

5. Into the largest puddle in the entire world.   _____

6. So that everyone will be friendly to us.   _____

7. Our car got a flat tire on the freeway.   _____

8. Because we promised her a bowl of ice cream after practice.   _____

9. My little girl performs with her aerial silks circus team.   _____

10. I promise to take you on a trip for your twelfth birthday.   _____

Phrases

A **phrase** is a group of words that does not contain both a subject and a verb.

THE PHRASE

A PREPOSITIONAL PHRASE
starts with a preposition and includes its object and any modifiers and can be used as an adjective or an adverb.

The chocolate **on the counter** belongs to me.

A PARTICIPIAL PHRASE
includes a participle (a verb acting as an adjective) and any modifiers and is used as an adjective.

I only eat chocolate **made by my sister.**

AN INFINITIVE PHRASE
*includes an infinitive (a verb form usually beginning with **to**) and any modifiers and can be used as an adjective, an adverb, or a noun.*

We want **to eat lots of chocolate.**

EXAMPLES

PREPOSITIONAL PHRASE
I accidentally threw my sandwich **out the window.**

Out the window acts as an adverb modifying the verb "threw."

PARTICIPIAL PHRASE
He gave me a sandwich recipe **written on an old napkin.**

Written on an old napkin acts as an adjective modifying "recipe."

INFINITIVE PHRASE
I need **to make another sandwich.**

To make another sandwich acts as the direct object of the verb "need."

Prepositional Phrases

Name:

A prepositional phrase includes the preposition, its object, and any of the object's modifiers.

A prepositional phrase can be used as an adjective or an adverb.

ADJECTIVE PHRASE

The box *of loud firecrackers* belongs to Dayton.

Of is the preposition, and *of loud firecrackers* is the prepositional phrase modifying the noun "box."

ADVERB PHRASE

The box of loud firecrackers belongs *to Dayton*.

To is the preposition, and *to Dayton* is the prepositional phrase modifying the verb "belongs."

Let's practice!

Instructions:
Underline the entire prepositional phrase in each of the sentences below and circle the preposition. Then indicate whether it is an adjective phrase or an adverb phrase.

EXAMPLE:

I dropped the extremely hot plate (on) the ground.   _____adverb_____

1.   That is the funniest joke I have heard in my life.   _____

2.   Please wash the dishes after dinner.   _____

3.   I choose the puppy in the corner.   _____

4.   Gibson's neighbor borrowed three cups of sugar.   _____

5.   The cat with orange and brown markings looks hungry.   _____

Your turn!

Instructions:
Incorporate the phrases below into complete sentences. Underline the phrase, and after the sentence, write ADJ if it's an adjective phrase and ADV if it's an adverb phrase.

1. in the world _____

2. beside the table _____

3. over the fence _____

Participial & Infinitive Phrases

A **participle** is a verb acting as an adjective. A **participial phrase** is always used as an adjective.

An **infinitive phrase** can be a subject, an object, or a predicate nominative.

PARTICIPIAL PHRASE

I only eat chocolate **made in Belgium**.

Made is a participle, and **made in Belgium** is the participial phrase acting as an adjective modifying "chocolate."

INFINITIVE PHRASE

I want **to eat chocolate**.

To eat chocolate is an infinitive phrase acting as the direct object of the verb, "want."

Let's practice!

Instructions:
Underline the participial or infinitive phrase in each of the sentences below. Then circle the participle or verb infinitive and indicate the type of phrase.

EXAMPLE:

<u>Thinking carefully</u>, Julian filled out the answers to the test.   participial

1. To be kind is the most important thing.   _____

2. This beautiful canyon, carved by the river, is worth the trip.   _____

3. The rooster crowing at sunrise always wakes me up.   _____

4. I always ask my friends to wash their hands.   _____

5. My main goal is to make as many friends as possible.   _____

Your turn!

Instructions:
Incorporate the phrases below into complete sentences. Underline the phrase, and after the sentence, write I if it's an infinitive phrase and P if it's a participial phrase.

1. to visit my friend _____

2. seen in New York _____

3. written by Julia _____

INSTRUCTIONS (PART ONE):

Practice using phrases by writing two complete sentences that incorporate each of the types of phrases below. Circle the phrase in each sentence.

PREPOSITIONAL PHRASE

1. _____

2. _____

PARTICIPIAL PHRASE

1. _____

2. _____

INFINITIVE PHRASE

1. _____

2. _____

INSTRUCTIONS (PART TWO):

Using one of the sentences above as the first sentence, write a story in which *every sentence includes a phrase.* Underline the phrase in each sentence, marking it as PREP, PART, or INF.

_____

_____

_____

_____

_____

_____

The Big "Phrases" Quiz!

INSTRUCTIONS: Underline any **prepositional phrases (PREP)**, **participial phrases (PART)**, and **infinitive phrases (INF)** in the sentences below and indicate the type of phrase in the space provided.

EXAMPLE:

My second cousin, Julian, loves <u>to make paper airplanes</u>.   _INF_

1. Laughing diabolically, the little girl stole my purse.   _____

2. Please put your shoes in the corner before you come inside.   _____

3. We watched the squirrels fight from a safe distance.   _____

4. To most people, rainy weather is not pleasurable.   _____

5. My grandmother only eats salsa made in Albuquerque.   _____

6. I think we all want to see that movie.   _____

7. Whatever you do, make sure to lock all the doors tonight.   _____

8. That dog doesn't know anything about road safety.   _____

9. I was scared when I saw my daughter tumbling down the stairs.   _____

10. My hometown, founded in 1803, is a lovely vacation spot.   _____

The Big Quiz Answer Key!

TYPES OF SENTENCES (p.13)

1. Interrogative
2. Declarative
3. Exclamatory
4. Declarative
5. Imperative
6. Interrogative
7. Imperative
8. Interrogative
9. Declarative
10. Exclamatory

SENTENCE STRUCTURES (p. 17)

1. Compound
2. Simple
3. Complex
4. Compound/ Complex
5. Complex
6. Simple
7. Compound
8. Complex
9. Complex
10. Simple

SUBJECTS (p. 22)

1. pancakes (S)
2. James, Buck, Yishan (C)
3. I (S)
4. people (S)
5. cats, dogs (C)
6. tests, quizzes (C)
7. pudding (S)
8. Someone (S)
9. boxes (S)
10. You, sister (C)

PREDICATES (p. 27)

1. yipped, chewed (C)
2. saw (S)
3. will be (S)
4. thought (S)
5. run, jog (C)
6. seems (S)
7. will bake (S)
8. Be, sit (C)
9. are (S)
10. watched, ate (C)

DIRECT OBJECTS (p. 32)

1. sister
2. stash
3. dishes
4. none
5. time
6. none
7. sound
8. effort
9. none
10. try

INDIRECT OBJECTS (p. 36)

1. me
2. none
3. myself
4. none
5. none
6. him
7. none
8. dog
9. us
10. cat

DIRECT & INDIRECT OBJECTS (p. 37)

1. DO: song, IO: me
2. DO: riddle, IO: kids
3. DO: truth, IO: none
4. DO: baseball, IO: me
5. DO: haircuts. IO: each other
6. DO: haircuts, IO: none
7. DO: none, IO: none
8. DO: glass, IO: everyone
9. DO: that, IO: none
10. DO: freedom, IO: ourselves

SUBJECT COMPLEMENTS (p. 43)

1. joker (PN)
2. actor (PN)
3. scratchy (PA)
4. rotten (PA)
5. person (PN)
6. serious (PA)
7. locked (PA)
8. hungry (PA)
9. sore (PA)
10. salesman (PA)

OBJECT COMPLEMENTS (p. 47)

1. none
2. Calla
3. none
4. happy
5. old-fashioned
6. traitor
7. black
8. healthy
9. captain
10. nervous

INDEPENDENT CLAUSES (p. 51)

1. Jay and Philip are good friends
2. none
3. I feel sorry for people
4. Gavin climbed up to my tree house / I was nowhere to be found
5. I didn't like the movie / the best part for me was the very end
6. Come here / sit down / be quiet
7. I am writing her a birthday card
8. Molly waited all night for the people across the street to turn off their lights and go to bed
9. I like cheese puffs / I don't enjoy chocolate mousse
10. none

SUBORDINATE CLAUSES (p. 57)

1. Whenever you feel like it (ADV)
2. who never even smiles at me (ADJ)
3. That we landed on the moon (N)
4. as soon as you get home (ADV)
5. that Avery would steal from her (N)
6. where they surfed all afternoon (ADJ)
7. If Xavier actually does his homework tonight (ADV)
8. that people in New Mexico ate so much green chile (ADJ)
9. because his little sister was about to barge into his room (ADV)
10. who gave me a chocolate bar (ADJ)

CLAUSES (p. 58)

1. Baxter watched (IND)
2. NOT
3. Susan, sister arrived (SUB)
4. Katherine, Vicky waited (IND)
5. NOT
6. everyone will be (SUB)
7. car got (IND)
8. we bought (SUB)
9. girl performs (IND)
10. I promise (IND)

PHRASES (p. 63)

1. Laughing diabolically (PART)
2. in the corner (PREP)
3. from a safe distance (PREP)
4. To most people (IND)
5. made in Albuquerque (PART)
6. to see that movie (INF)
7. to lock all the doors tonight (INF)
8. about road safety (PREP)
9. down the stairs (PREP)
10. founded in 1803 (PART)

CPSIA information can be obtained
at www.ICGtesting.com
Printed in the USA
JSRC021159111020
JK10393900001B/1

9 781644 420195